Michelene Wandor is a p[...] broadcaster. Her dramatisati[...] Wandering Jew was staged a[...] prolific work for radio includes dramatisations of *Persuasion* and *Pride and Prejudice, Kipps, The Brothers Karamazov, The Moonstone* and *Hemlock and After*. Her adaptation of *The Belle of Amherst*, from the play by William Luce, won Thames TV an International Emmy Award.

Michelene Wandor's books on theatre include *Carry on Understudies*, about theatre and sexual politics, and *Look Back in Gender: The Family and Sexuality in Postwar British Drama*.

Gardens of Eden
Revisited

CONTENTS

Gardens of Eden

Eve and Lilith have a private word

After Winter Poems

Other Poems

Gardens
of Eden

Eve, in the morning

So God created man (sic) in his (sic) own image?

'Male and female he created them'   *Genesis 1:27*

Look
it was only a tree, for God's sake
a nice tree
nice shade, green leaves
an apple

You eat one apple and they remember you forever; you
only want to be left in peace, make
chutney, compote, dried apple rings
on a string

a snake? don't be silly
knowledge? you read too many Good Books
naked? so I like the sun. I tan easy

Hava. Eve. Me

Sarah, Abraham's wife, the mother of Israel?
Well, let me tell you
you
couldn't tell
my chicken soup
from hers

you work your ribs to the bone
setting up the human race
and do you get any thanks?
a *nächtige tug* you get thanks
for freezing in
a goddam garden

I was glad we had to move, get
a decent place
those ants everywhere
and I mean everywhere

well, I've got a lot of grandchildren now
a little too much begetting, maybe
but as long as they've got their health and strength

I was always a good mother
no one can say I wasn't
a good mother.

Lilith, in the morning

abstract art must truly be divine
for did not the Lord say

'thou shalt not make unto
thee any graven images or any likeness
of any thing that is in heaven above
or that is in the earth beneath
or that is in the water under the earth'   *Exodus 20:4*

gold and silver and brass
blue   purple   scarlet   linen
goat's hair
            oil for light   spices for anointing   oil
incense   onyx
                        emerald   sapphire
diamond   agate   amethyst

blue lace
            bread and lamb

4

my burnt offerings
my tabernacle, my temple: art

myrrh   cinnamon
olive oil

frankincense
                         stone tablets
pillars of cloud and fire

shining faces
almonds   flowers

oh God

Eve has a problem

what should I do?

the boys, Cain and Abel, they fight
fight, fight, all the time

what can you do?

I keep busy.

Lilith and guilt

a burnt offering, that's me
my blood sprinkled about
the altar of Adam's rib

no blood, no fat, thin and pale
I, the sacrificial lamb
flung out of heaven
because the Law
was made against me

when you are a burnt offering
you must atone and atone

for what sin? for what crime?

pillars of fire, salty, smoke
rancid
join the unclean, the hare
the camel the swine the prawn
the eagle the crab the raven
and the owl and the owl and the owl

touch me and you will go unclean
even unto my dead body
you may try to purify me, sprinkle my blood
at the foot of the altar
burn my sweet flesh for a sin offering
and still you will be unclean
you can never wash me away
I am the devil that haunts

I am neither cloven-hoofed
nor do I chew the cud

therefore you must break me, like an earthenware vessel

you may wash your clothes
till the fibres melt
into your skin, and still
you will be
unclean

for I
am the devil
that haunts

Eve and Lilith in a garden

cloud by day and fire by night
lungs clog damp by day
burn sharp by night
eyes will not close

no sleep

Mother Eve make a fire, sweet
woodsmoking streaks breath
deep with smart freshness

Lilith changes the wind's direction
with a blink
clouds the sweetness with
acrid flashes, Eve
faces, eyes angry, Lilith signals
to her not to limit
the possibilities of fire
Lilith makes her cough, her eyes
look down, modest with pain

milk and honey stand curdled
and hard
between them

perhaps a stick with flowers on it
is needed
to prove healing?

perhaps a proper diet
might
do the trick

Eve to Lilith

don't get me wrong —
I have nothing against
first wives

ok, so you laid him first; that's merely
a fact of life
so you got to know
all his little habits, like
picking his nose
when he reads in bed

he didn't do that with you?
I see

I'm not jealous. I don't
believe in jealousy, and
what I don't believe in
doesn't hurt me. But tell me
honestly, what did you do to the poor man?
He's a nervous wreck.
He can't stand up to his boss, he has
pains in his side all the time —
I mean, something must have happened
to leave a man
so scarred.

He's told me how beautiful you were.
The dark, dramatic type.

Usually he doesn't talk about you
but when we — well, long ago —
when — at night —
we — in the dark, always —
he used to call your name
at a certain moment.

It's none of my business
but you must have done
something very special
to make a man
remember you so

Lilith to Eve

I merely said 'no'.

That's when he gave me
his attention
for the first time

9

Lilith finds a book

Moses forty days and forty nights

forty years of some other hunger
in the wilderness
before I came upon
the Great Book, chapter
versed, marching columns deep
clenched each number, phase

I find laws:
two wives a man can have
kill a woman's parents, shave
her head, pare her nails
give her a mouth to mourn
and then fuck her: thus
the chosen tribe chooses

don't dress in each other's clothes

die if you are a virgin
die if you sleep with another man
die if you sleep with a woman
stone you if you are a whore

if he doesn't like you, he
can write his divorce down
and you may go

if your husband dies, his
brother can have you
keep it in the family

and still I see
                amethyst   agate

blue lace and spices
and Sarah, mother of Israel, smiling at me

but seven times round what city?
causing whose walls to fall?

Lilith seeks a quest

Deborah
here
judges Israel, a prophetess
under her tree

Jael hammers the nail into Sisera's temple
his head on the ground, now
forever doomed to listen
to the earth

Deborah sings, to see
such fun
and she hugs Jael

Oh, I am bitter for my sin of simple being

I would not be a priest for anything

when I bleed my flowers be upon me or my man
he is unclean
when I bear
I am unclean
when I take his seed into me
I am unclean
I must atone and separate from my uncleanness
I must not eat blood
for it is the life of all flesh
he must not see me naked, for I am his
nakedness

if blood and life and nakedness
cannot meet in one flesh, where
is holiness?

there is something unfinished
that is holy, a grape in the corner of the vineyard, for the
poor to eat

it is hard to love my neighbour
as myself

Lilith chooses a quest

women fight, women prophesy, women
lead, women judge

when Samson is born
Delilah becomes the betrayer of strength
Deborah is delighted

Eve gives counsel

Jael,
why don't you take up a hobby?
I hear carpentry's very
popular with girls nowadays.

Delilah, hairdressing would suit
you. A little skill with the scissors
would do no harm.

Deborah, for God's sake
stop
all that giggling.

Eve and Lilith make a pact

Eve: What are we fighting over?

Lilith: I don't know.

Eve: Is it a man?

Lilith: Is it a book?

Eve: It might be a man.

Lilith: I don't think so.

Eve: Is it a garden?

Lilith: Perhaps so.

Eve: Perhaps it's the world.

Lilith: I don't know.

Eve: If we don't know,
         we'd better look.
         I'll take the world.

Lilith: I'll take the book.

Eve: Come on. I'll show you around.

Ruth's story, as told to Lilith

She was left with two sons.
They they too died and we, their wives, strangers
to her blood, remained: Orpah and I, Ruth. My name
like anger, my temperament to match: passion
it would be called, if
roused to love or fury.

I don't know why I loved her;
simply to follow
Naomi was all I desired.
I even rose to the heights
of poetry: 'Whither thou goest,' said I,
'I will go; where thou lodgest, I will lodge,
thy people shall be my people
and thy God my God.
Where thou diest, will I die
and there will I be buried.'

Not so much did I promise her son
in my heart, my husband.

I have been a stranger
all my life.

We returned to Bethlehem
with the barley harvest, Naomi
calling herself Mara, she who is
bitter.

For bread I gleaned
corn in Boaz' field, dusted
golden sheaves in the setting sun.

Well, one thing leads to another
and Naomi's husband's land
passed to the hand
of Boaz, and I with it.
Such is the scythe that comes between women.

Naomi dances my child now, and
the line continues. Sheaves smile
in her iris eyes when she looks at me. They say I am
better to her than
seven sons had been. They do not
know how much I love her, more
than I could seven sons.

I am still a stranger.

Eve's commentary

Ruthie, I'd like
to give you the benefit
of my advice:

you should never get too
involved
with a mother-in-law.

Lilith in court

two harlots, they were
(what you and I would now call
two single mothers)
                    the two alone one night (as usual)

one baby died
its mother swapped it with the living
and Solomon in his supposed wisdom
forced the truth into the open
(apparently)

as though the dead child's mother
would have time for anything
but howling grief, as though
another's child
could replace the cooling warmth in her heart

Lilith knows: I have had
many children and sent them
all forth to people the air

in court
the mothers laughed
in Solomon's face, to see a man
suppose that any woman's grief
could so craze her
that she would see
another child
put to death

a mother becomes a jealous god to
avenge her child

not to destroy for the sake
of an act of will, let alone
for a cheap moral ending

Eve's commentary

be fair; you're
taking it all a
little bit
too literally

what about Solomon's proverbs?
there's an achievement

Lilith reads the proverbs

three thousand proverbs
and songs one thousand and five, beneath
whose shade I may dream:

cedar trees
           from Lebanon   fir trees

a temple of wood, warm cedar
and gold   olive trees
                      hard wood

seven years

two hundred pomegranates
                    lilies

lions   oxen   cherubim

gold candlesticks
           hinges of gold

the glory of the Lord comes on a gold cloud

followed by plagues, pestilences and locusts

Eve has some gossip

They say
Jezebel slew the prophets.

It's rubbish.
She was with me all the time.

Lilith's meditations

One

fire comes down from heaven
and consumes men — just
like that

how many miracles can a woman do?
give birth
bleed
love

and with all these miracles
still seem
unclean

what more must she do? conjure up chariots of fire?
horses of fire?

should she smite the waters, that they
might part (*pace* Elijah)?

turn children into bears?

no

obey   obey   obey

this is her impossible miracle

Jezebel, eaten by dogs
for doing nothing
that I can fathom
merely what she was told

only her skull
her feet
and the palms of her hands left
all the better to see you with
sockets follow you
bloody hands touch you
her blood sprinkled on your bread

someone has bad dreams

Two

the miracles are the best
columns of fire and salt and cloud
even a plague from nowhere
fills dying nostrils
with sweet incense

there is no peace in the Old Testament
all rush and worry, worry and rush

a broken Bible poises
my palm, my left
palm, whole and warm

a house filled with a cloud

Lilith mourns with Nehemia, the man with a soul

what with smiting and weeping
and fasting and mourning
and plagues and diseases

and sinning and corrupting and
sinning
and corrupting
and sackcloth
and seed
and all that begetting
and the smell
and burnt offerings

Eve's commentary

enough to make anyone
welcome
Jesus and penicillin
with open arms, eh?

Eve takes a trip

the soup's on a low flame
clean socks and shirts
in the cupboard

I breathed polish on the candlesticks
I dusted the incense

butter's in the freezer
chopped liver in the
pottery dish covered with cling-film

all you need to buy
each day
is bread and fruit

the biscuit tin is full
and there's a new
packet of matza
on the top shelf

I'm taking some ham
and pickle sandwiches
on rye

expect me when you see me

Lilith re-tells Esther's story

the world rustles for Esther
in her best red weave

only nine chapters, she has
little time to coin a magic mine

meanwhile, back at the palace, King Ahasuerus
feasts the men, while meanwhile
behind the palace, Queen Vashti
feasts the women.

Vashti is summoned to the king's presence
but being rosy with the jokes
of women, she puts her foot down

fuck off, you wally (or some Old Testament
equivalent), I won't be shown off like
a prize cow this time

the lads, of course, don't take to that at all
because everyone knows that once a queen
sets a bad eg
any woman could take it into her
head to disobey
her lord and master

get rid of Vashti, advise
the princes, fear seaming their pores,
replace her with another — after all, every man
should bear rule
in his own house

so King A orders a load
of virgins (what's so special
about virgins?) from whom
to choose a replacement
for Vashti

meanwhile, back in the ghetto
Mordecai, the Jew, hears of this and sends
his cousin Hadassah (Esther to you)
along with the other virgins, and lo,
she is chosen with a select few
for further tests (the king conveniently
unaware of her ethnic origins)

a year of 'purification'; oil of
myrrh, sweet odours, and one by one,
in turn, in turn, the young women
are set before the king
for him to try
till he gets bored

Esther, however, does not bore him
at all, and as her reward, King A
sets the crown upon her head
and her body in his bed
Mordecai meanwhile hovers round the gate

also meanwhile, a bad man called Haman
becomes King A's right-hand man,
a misnomer for such a sinister man
who likes all
to bow down
before him

Mordecai, always a meanwhile man,
refuses to bow, and in revenge Haman
decides to kill all
the Jews (where
have we heard that one since?)

anyway, the long and the short of it is that
Esther so continues to please King A
with her courage and her beauty
that Haman is sussed out
and hanged
the Jews are saved
and Mordecai rises
to be second-in-command
to King A

there is something missing
from this story:
someone
somewhere
doesn't bother to say
whether Esther
actually liked
King A

Eve visits Rome

Pope Joan

A lady pope?

Who gets pregnant?

Do me a favour.

Lilith comforts Job

poor Job
you did try

but finally you freaked and cursed
as would anyone whose sheep
were burned, whose body was covered
in boils

you did not, of course,
know of the bet
God and Satan were
waging over your soul

you tried saying 'the Lord
giveth and the Lord taketh away
blessed be the Lord'

but there came a point
where it just
didn't sound right

all you wanted was justice
a fair fight
God to face you face to face
not simply strike
from behind a cloud

no one likes a moody man
no one likes another's anger

they came from all sides
telling you to pray
to keep your good counsel
to believe   to believe   to believe
but you stuck to your guns
could not cease questioning.
would not abandon your integrity

you asked for help for them that
have no power, for
those with no strength to be saved
for if God was truly with you, you argued,
then God would cast you out if you pretended to
be other than you were

'the price of wisdom is above rubies,' you said
Job 28:18

but of course
in the end
after the Lord
has spent chapters challenging you
to a competition
of creation and power

of course you repented

who can compete with a man
who creates a world
in seven days?

Eve visits Greece 1

One: Persephone alone

like a finger-tip gliding over
ivory, I
smooth my evening

once more in harmony, I sit
among familiars: white
daisies under my hands, my
curtain of swinging hair a
band of lace

here I can remember
that the seventh note
is always sharp; the seventh
month the time of my leaving,
the seventh day a small plateau
of rest

here I am invisible
no mother
no dark lord
here I spike stars
on my knuckles
kick rainbows
like dry leaves in autumn

here I stitch my plans
and knit
my revolution

here, in the house of anonymity
I love myself
I am defiant as cactus
I am unnamed, per se,
Persephone peeled pitted
towards an obligation
she chooses

Lilith on first love

well, you were
my evil eye, you
came along with your
on-the-road mentality
you were
a play with name unspeakable
you
beckoned me, an innocent
to superstition's grip

a drum, a drum beat
my heart wild, no witch's
cauldron could draw me
from your corporeal eye
no ritual exorcism
keep me from
your name dreamed,
a real man
with no need to beckon
me on, just the being
enough.
         Lilith, you
called me. I, your name,
never spoke

Eve visits Greece 2

Two: a statue

head   red   fronds

friends, they might have —
                                        a red flag

feast his eyes, he could not:
a stone, his head, perhaps

his eyes black pips, spat
out by the snakes, her hair

only wings on his heels, not
his mind

Perseus, Medusa;
lovers they might have been
but when he looked at her
he thought he saw
snakes where her hair

she, pinned below him,
reaches
to caress his leg
feels wings at his ankle flutter
with fear

her marble breast beats
below his foot
his sword shielding his guilt

a moment, and
her neck cracks
green and white marble melon
in the square, water
marble   melon

pink shy outer layer, fury
passion-tongued, squirms
in his hand, foams over her
rose heart

Eve meets Medusa

Medusa. Sit down. Take
the weight off your snakes. We have
a lot in common. Snakes, I mean.

Tell me, can you really turn men
to stone with a look? Do you
think, if I had a perm —
maybe not.

Don't you think
Perseus was
a bit of a coward? not even
to look you in the face

you were beautiful when you
were a moon goddess, before
Athene changed your looks
through jealousy

I can't see what's wrong
with making love
in a temple, even
if it was her temple

it's a good mask; you must
feel safe and loving
behind it

you must feel very powerful

tell me, what conditioner do you use?

Lilith takes tea with the Lord

One

'the Lord knoweth the way
of the righteous
but the way of the ungodly
shall perish'   *Psalms 1:16*

how do you recognise an enemy?
leave it to the Lord: he knows

but I cannot act out of someone
else's knowledge

tell me, why
should you have a monopoly
on anger and rage, revenge
and punishment

what about me

32

ok, so you made heaven and earth
and the stars   so?
no one
asked you, did I ask you, I wasn't even made, how
could I ask you?

anyway, you're only interested in man (sic)
you put all things under his feet, including women
and still you expect gratitude

let me tell you, Lord,
your characters are taking over
you will fall into the ditch you are digging

I searched for a joyful psalm, to let me
praise and praise
instead I am beginning to feel
crabby again, oh Lord
why do I bother

what about us being nice
to each other?

you fly upon the wings of the wind
you hail stones and coals of fire
you shoot arrows of lightning
and the breath from your nostrils
burns

you have all the good bits
and I scare easy

Two

you are as a bridegroom
coming out of your chamber, rejoicing as a
strong man to run a race

ever macho, eh, Lord

there's a thing I'd like
to say
I am not happy when I am afraid
and if I am simply to fear you, then
I must be unhappy, right?
what pleasure do you get

from unhappy people
what *nachas*?

remember when you said, 'fight
against them that fight against me'
that struck a chord:
                    for if they that without cause
have hid for me their net in a pit,
then shall their net that they have hid
catch themselves unawares, then indeed
my soul will be joyful and rejoice
in your salvation

I want to be my own jealous God, you see

for the irony is,
I am made only too well
in thine image, the
image of a jealous God *(see Psalm 35)*

'the meek shall inherit the earth?'
I have not learned meekness from watching you

34

you have made me
the heathen in my own heart
I have invaded myself
I am a stranger in my midst
I do not belong to myself

I dream that the
wings of a dove might suit me
soft, loving peace calling
unto me, and I could fly away, far

but your tongue is a sharp sword
your teeth spears
and my heart a snapped string

you give me yourself with one hand
and with the other
you take me away
how the hell do I know
where the hell
I am

I could play music for you
I could sing my poems for you
I could make you laugh
I could learn to make soup, knit
a coat of many colours for you

but I will not sit in sackcloth
will not dry my palms with ashes
will not eat the dust
for that does not celebrate you
and that does not celebrate me
and I am into fairness
which means we must both
get enough out of it
a little word
reciprocity

you say you will hover over me
your wings
giving me protection
I've got news for you
I'm allergic to feathers

Three

yes, you did do some nice things
silver and gold, water and fire
bread and quails
and *matza brei*

must have been a lot of work
proof-reading the tablets
(keep taking the tablets,
I hear myself think;
sorry, Lord)

I did sit down by the
waters of Babylon
and wept
oh, I wept so much

when I sat down it
was a gentle flow
and when I got up
after weeping
there they were,
the waters of Babylon
my waters
my tears that made a stream
a river

a sea

Eve comforts Lilith, from afar

'every wise woman buildeth her house'   *Proverbs 14:1*

excuse me, Lord
I have to take delivery
of some bricks

Lilith faces the dark night of her soul

a dry person, broken
into many selves

I am rigid with
the fear of dust

a dry person, a
woman who hacks girders
against green hillsides
stacking old moments
on an open palm

she hears through stone walls
she craves you
she shells your skull hollow
on the outside
you need not go far
to think, she surprises you

she is stainless, hurt
brushes off her

a dry person
rinses you away
a solid swirling mist
into a dark nowhere
a dry person
always sees the sky
a dry person
darkens the ground
at your feet, rocks
your shape
the dry woman turns
ash, stings
your instep, clings
under your eyelids

you cannot lean into the hill
for the dry woman will stone you
lean into the valley
she will push you

she is a hollow wind
jumping at your back
she tries to shield from you
your knowledge
that you must grow
where you fall

Eve visits Greece 3

Three: Andromeda's turn

Perseus is a tomorrow
sort of person, dashing fresh
from killing an unseen
Medusa to
save Andromeda

hell is yesterday's pit, fixed in fear
of someone who once helped her
to do good —
a monster good at fixing
a lavatory cistern, and she knew
she wasn't bothered by looks as such:
the 'monster' was a man who listened

Andromeda now, a peach stone
against rock's flesh
wrists rasp and back skins
against a cliff
which everyone fears (hence ideal
for sacrifice, thinks the village)

an angry sea, grey with hunger
no fish in its belly
for months
no bread
for days
so a quick-fathomed decision
was taken
based on the waves
in her hair, amber waves
to taunt the raging grey

they grabbed her in the middle
of a cup of nectar, peach juice
staining her chin, can't
reach to lick it up, won't let
her use the back of her hand

when she was a child
Andromeda dreamed
of gracing a powerful man, handsome,
feared by everyone, godlike, even;

now she curses her misunderstood arrogance
and waits for the winged beauty
to save her from
her one chance of heaven

Lilith looks in the mirror

My skin is silk, my tongue is wine
my teeth are sunlight
my nails are fine linen

when I walk
I sail like a ship
in a fresh wind

I am beautiful
and need not be told so

I belong to no one
and my own works
praise me in the gates

the word 'virtue' is not
in my vocabulary
'strength' is

Eve, alone

when you're tired
you cry

the sky has been tired
for days

Lilith looks ahead

'there is no new thing under the sun'   *Ecclesiastes 1:9*

you may have to
cloud your sun
for what I say
is new

to every thing there is a season
and a time
to every purpose
under the heaven
a time to be born
and a time to die
a time to plant
and a time to pluck up that which is planted
a time to kill
and a time to heal

41

a time to weep and a time to laugh
a time to mourn
and a time to dance

a time to embrace
and a time
to refrain from embracing

a time to get
and a time to lose
a time to keep
and a time to cast away
a time to rend
and a time to sew
a time to keep silence
and a time to speak

a time to love
and a time to hate
a time of war
and a time of peace

best is the sight of the eyes
and the wandering of desire

and then who dares say
that sorrow is better than laughing

for now there is a thing
that's new, a thing
that brings
its own season   .

not only man is wise
not only woman the ensnarer

evil, madness and death:
them will I live among
but by them be not touched

if I eat my bread with joy
and my wine with a merry heart
it is because I
have seen happiness, have heard
joy and know what
I have seen and heard

my eyes are not vanity
my ears are not vanity
my skin is not vanity

I will not fear
that which I cannot see
that which I cannot hear

I will even welcome bad dreams

Eve seeks refuge

my feet are killing me; rope
sandals and leaf mulch don't mix
and a forest is a hard
path when you're not as fit
as you were

a hut   suspended in the air

stilts?   tripods?   magic?
feet   legs   chicken legs
three chicken legs. A hut
on three chicken legs.

a door — open
a fire — burning
yeast, a hot loaf, crusty from the oven
tea   a samovar steaming
a chair   cushions

paradise; this is the garden of Eden

Baba Yaga flies above me,
rows her way through clouds
sweeps her flight path away
with her broom, besom-brisk, soars
and swoops and sweeps and sways
and when she's lonely her
chicken legs run her home
to another part of the forest

Baba, never bored, ever busy

Baba — buba — someone lost,
something heavy, a heavy
wanting — a mother — and who
was Eve's mother?

a mother who sweeps trouble
away, wipes tears, is always
there, in spirit if not in apron

Baba flies
Baba twists
Baba has no house of gingerbread
but a sturdy shelter
Baba is not evil
but powerful
Baba waves and flies

Baba has a meal set out for me
a bed warming for me
a loom weaving for me
porridge just right for me
Baba writes a book for me
paints pictures on my eyelids
warms my hands in hers

Baba touches me gently
on the shoulder
tells me
it's time
to move on

Lilith dreams

the Lord rocks me to sleep
makes sure I have his dreams
and then protests
when I wake
from a nightmare

Eve decides to return

There's something about
the quiet of your own front door
that makes it musical
after absence

Lilith thinks about loving

a sort of neg-
ative push   the valley
spins cupidity

I lie, sucking earth,

stones gravel my lips
granite strokes my cheek

I have been sour, eaten
with hate, I admit it
I have no more shame

the ground has spat me
forth, frothed me
at its corners

I curl and hammer
flat my hands   palm splat blades
green my fingers

seeping a late dew softens me
my hand on my face
I might learn to forgive

Eve wanders in another glade

here
a Narcissus
who traded in his manhood
in order to spend all day
recognising himself

here
Peter Pan

who traded in his manhood
in order to avoid
recognising himself

neither grew up

on the edge of the pool
Echo shivers with guilt: all
she did was show him
(Narcissus)
she loved him
by giving him back his words

by the front door
Wendy stands
puzzled
all she did was show him
(Peter Pan)
how much she loved him
by warming his slippers

Adam, does any of this
ring a bell?

Lilith's dance

Lilith sins?

Lilith sings
Lilith speaks many a cross word
Lilith has an anger like love
like a procession of pillars
of fire
Lilith has the delight
of a woman scorned

he modelled me
I was his clay thing
into me he breathed life
I became his *golem*
I went forth and I destroyed
havoc my middle name

I am the *dybbuk* of delight
I slip into the souls
of those who need me

perhaps you breathed
just a little
too much life, a sniffle too long
but once tasting the air
I would not be still, not
be silent, not return
to my feet of clay

I will not gather dust
I do not cower beneath cobwebs
I do not fear the hot streets

I walk
in the middle
of the pavement

I do not hug the shade
of cowardly buildings
I do not stay in my ghetto
but I strut and stride
into the ghetto
of men
I interrupt
the invisible universal
which denies men their souls
and women their being

I do not creep

I do not crawl

see

I am proud

I have taken the cloth
from my mirror
of mourning

for your birthday
(if gods have birthdays)
I shall give you
a mirror

Eve remembers birth

the first stage

looking skywards
night dusts
eyes shell light
dark husks darkness

the second stage

the ship has rocked silently
now sense the wind waving
someone billows
translucence
at night havens hum, a slow, soft
ticking, lazy between
curling surf

the third stage

the whale in the womb
finger-thrusts starwise out
nudge-noses soft horizons
glistens and dances
grows and softens
sleeks a path
to a cold, edgy awakening
and the discovery
of a warm love
that begins to
compensate

Lilith flies

glass night protects
you, flying high
above
pestilences and plagues:

from a great height
blood shines, and
locusts carve poems
out of clouds

your children fly round
you, their wings cooling
and warming by turns, they
breathe fire and salt

their shining faces
are spice and song

you smile

Eve prepares

I have passed over from
my Egypt
into the world

I have eaten the bread of strangers
who became friends

I have slept in the houses
of others, and listened
to decisions
that became mine

I have found that my world
can sit on my back, a cross
between Atlas and a snail,
the strength of both
and the delicacy
of both

I have found that sleep can come
anywhere
that warmth can be built
that the world is larger than one garden

I am preparing, therefore,
the first dinner
to which I shall invite
the family of my choice

the forest gave me a tree, with thick strong
green needles
when I carried it across
my threshold, the sharp greenness
turned shimmer-silver, a thousand
shadows in light, slim and flat, a
transparent tree which shines shadow
into winter light

some invitations

Jael is carving me a large table

Deborah has promised not to pass judgement
on the dinner, unless it's praise

Delilah is planning to dye her
hair green, to go
with the new curtains
and the tree

Ruth and Naomi are bringing
a double sleeping-bag

Pope Joan can leave the baby
in my bedroom; Solomon's
two lady friends are bringing
their babies too
Perseus and Peter Pan will
amuse the children with flying tricks

The Queen of Sheba is dropping
in after dinner
for a cognac

Jezebel can leave the dogs outside

Esther and Vashti will bring the
book they are writing together, and
doubtless argue all the way
through dinner

Persephone is bringing her mother;
they can sit opposite one another

Medusa and her Gorgon sisters
are going to play a trio for recorders

Andromeda is bringing some seaweed,
chinese-style-fried

Baba Yaga and Sarah are both
bringing chicken soup

Wendy is just going
to enjoy herself
for a change

and that nice girl Judy, from
Chicago, who is very fond of
dinner parties,
is coming

that's a lot of guests; a lot
of *kneidlach*

the dinner

I am lighting candles in memory
because they give a beautiful light
and a candle will always
look you in the eye, straight

ritual is a good thing
everything in order, everything
ordered, a Seder, an order
to events, courses of action
and an order for eating

here, of course, is the empty
place, the space for
the uninvited guest, a prophet,
a strange Elijah, a dark,
vibrant woman

to drink a cup of sweet red wine
a silver cup for her, a cup
with no stem, no handle
to be clasped between both hands, a goblet
of sparkling hope

the absent friend,
awaited

Eve to Lilith

your mouth is a pomegranate
ripening in smile

I can see into the garden
my sister, my love

I have mixed you a banana milk shake
milk to make your bones strong
banana to make the adrenalin
course through your blood

your throat is a white pillar
I stand and watch you drink
I am swimming into your heart
your cheeks are a bed of spices
your eyes are bay leaves
your legs are pillars of marble

you are too thin
come into my kitchen

Lilith to Eve

you hide your face
let me touch you
your skin is soft as peaches
your hand a gentle lily

your shoulders are the slopes
of Lebanon
your arms the strong cedars
the mist of your breath
is home

you are blue lace
and spices

Eve's poem

We must go in.
The others are waiting.

Eve and Lilith
have a private word

Lilith, the poem

Lilith is not a reason
Lilith is not a cause
Lilith is not an inspiration
Lilith
is

When I was ten
we had a cat
and I called her Lilith
she was black
with white paws
a white ruff
and white strips running between
her two fore feet
and her two back feet

my mother told me later
that I had wanted to call her Lilith
she did not know why
I could not remember why

Lilith was cool
aloof
friendly only to me
she spat and scratched
but I would not let her be
and persuaded her
against all the world's odds
that I loved her
and in return
she loved me

She had two litters of kittens
that I remember
and all were given away
or disappeared

after the third litter she was
sad and slow
hiding with her kittens
behind a pile of sacking
only allowing me near her with food and milk
when the last kitten had gone
she walked away across the fields
she never came back

Lilith, the cat
the mother

many years later I began
writing poems
and Lilith sometimes
showed her face
I did not know why
I cannot remember why

many years later
I discovered I was allergic to cats
many years later
I became a mother

Lilith, the mother
the cat

and many years later
my mother died
and shortly after that
I began
re-reading the Good Book
and found that it felt as
familiar as a cat's fur
and as infuriating as a rash

and I began to answer back
late at night
when no one was awake
and two voices spoke
and one of them was kind
and caring and fed up
and the other was dark and glittering
and brave
and fed up

and when the reading was ended
after months
and the voices were sprawled
over pages
I gave the voices names
and they were called Eve and Lilith

and the one could not be without the other
the cat and the mother

Eve was the cornerstone of the Good Book
(for had she not 'sinned'
it would never have been written)
the world owes her everything

Lilith was never even a runner for the Good Book
having transgressed before sinning was a crime
Lilith, the cat, the mother
the female Lucifer

Eve's children people the world
Lilith is never allowed to keep her children

Eve cares about everyone
Lilith cares about art

Eve is never alone
Lilith cannot rely on anyone

Eve has never had the luxury
of a dark night of the soul
Lilith has never known her own hearth

the two women meet for the first time ever
in Gardens of Eden

where they cultivate new plants
and find there are alternatives
to being fed up

this is the story of Lilith
who cannot exist without Eve

Lilith is spiky
and can be as tall as Cruella de Ville
in Walt Disney's
'Hundred and One Dalmatians'
Lilith is still black and white
Lilith can still spit and scratch
Lilith can look into your heart
and your soul
and release angels and demons
Lilith will love you
and frighten you
with her love

and when
in the warm limbo of night
Lilith curls alone
on a soft cloud
the vapour floats warm and steamy
round her
and she weeps
for she cannot understand
why her beauty
makes others fear her

Eve comforts her
from afar
with tea
and vodka
and brings the spark back to her eye

she sleeps
to wake another day

Eve finds tears
and Lilith finds a friend

a deal

say the women to each other

knowing that clouds drift in many shapes
a cat, a mother, a book

Lilith goes to Kol Nidrei

after the smudged, grubbed marble
where no flower blooms
and three stones flower
in shadow,
a name is sadly missed
because of the smile
to which it once belonged

tonight he suddenly appears
as a god of compassion
shedding the lord of revenge
who accompanies Elijah
after the chicken soup

tonight he suggests we all forgive
one another
and tonight
he suggests in passing
that forgiveness must be mutual
as confession must be mutual

aha! I was awake
and caught that
it lets me off the *goyische* hook
turn the other cheek?
never
never did
never will

never will never fail
turn the other cheek
and call it masochism

admit you're wrong
and might be forgiven
might is the strongest possibility
after all,
I may forget
but I never forgive

is that what you meant, lord?
the question is rhetorical

After Winter
Poems

A poem for the mountain

see-saw
the trees
see-saw
the skis
saw-see
the children
pile snow-sand
in snow-suits
and saw-see
the red jackets
pile down
the piste
while see-saw
above
the gondola
hovers
before
home and
pain chocolat
sees

A poem for snow

in between
the running
and
the silk
cloud descends
water cools
and white
sneaks
around
hidden peaks

A poem for the rain

snow
it
ain't

A poem for promises

taking it from here
into thuggery
a diamond rasps
its clasp
into throaty lines
where lying hurts
more than any bruise
because the past
is recast
as one question after another

A poem for walking

when umbrellas
drip
it is time
for the boots
to
proof themselves

A poem for inspiration

stomach
rumbles
sometimes
before
sometimes
after
sometimes
during

A poem for bananas

half
have
now
and have
half
later

A poem on work

a poem
is
and can be
work
and a poem
can
work
and
work
can be
sheer poetry

A poem for glaciers

grit and growl
says the salad bowl
with wood grain
that wouldn't
poison a fairy
with its weave
and weft

follow the cut
dark and shining
till it looks like
a spool
that backwards
flies like
cloud spume
whose formation
lies

A poem on mountain streams

it may
be easy
to walk on
water
but writing
a torrent
is quite
another
water bed

A poem for chamois

the goat
thought
its horns
were
a dilemma
on
the mountain

A poem for clouds

a misty moment
squeezes the valley
invisible
saving up
revenge

A poem for dawn

the mist
nets the sun
so that
only the gathers
swing
in the breeze

the least you can do
is collect
yourself
in colour

the nets mist the sun
catching
troubling motes
which might
read
more light
than their day
gives

A poem for wheels

driving snows
slide blades
for grass chains
and upright
branches
make the metal
machine
safe
as
warm houses

A poem for lunch

hash browns
where
no hash fires
while summer
green
salads
through a
glass
bowl
springly

A poem for eating

later
the capon
will emerge
while first
the carrot
soups

A poem for drinking

the sound
of wine
chinks
and clinks
its taste
around
the table

A poem for the horizon

like a
noticing finger
distance
fastens easily
on some
more minds
than others

at least
so timetables
think

A poem for dinner

rice rises
to green leaf
memories
and
yesterday's
caper
at the
table

A poem for masks

green glow
the eyes through
fingers
smooth and
purifying
and red apples
taste
sweet

A poem for the impossible

asking
is not taking
though asking
can lead to
giving

A poem for wolves

a wood
wolves
with wild horses
and a guitar
twanging
in the
wind

A poem for strings

pull 'em
bow 'em
tie 'em
cut 'em
change 'em
no string
unstrung

A poem for a door

squeak and slide
over stone
bang and latch
and shower clean
where soft towels
wait blue
and precious
for a project
and a year
when something

A poem for sleeping

bed

Other Poems

Antigone 1

Antigone with Oedipus
another kind of Cordelia
to another kind of Lear

she sees the city for him
she softens the rock with her voice
she, no stranger to devotion

she guides, Oedipus makes the speeches

Antigone, a good girl since womanhood
did not sit meekly at home to sew
but chose the wild, to sew
comfort for blind Oedipus

Ismene, her sister, remained within four walls
to sew
it is she who brings news of their
brothers' strife

Polynices banished and Eteocles
(who always grabbed the best grapes)
stayed within the walls of Thebes

Antigone has her hands full, what with
a fire for night, water
to wash Oedipus' wounds, air
to plan for the day

she pleads that Oedipus speak
to Polynices, the family that ties together
flies together
she rushes between father and son, oh yes, noble, oh yes,
brave

and yet and yet

my daughters have been loyal to me,
says Oedipus; they
are my sons

Antigone pleads with Polynices
to turn his army back — why fight your brother? what
mess
of pottage is at stake

she knows that it is spelled pride, that
faces fall and are lost in such battles
Antigone has always loved Polynices' face, the full
lips that laugh so easily, the lion's
profile, the confident thighs

Antigone is being uneconomical: asking
a lot of questions and
getting no answers
no one asks her anything

Antigone 2

Only Theseus saw Oedipus die; his
daughters ('sons'?) barred
from watching
only women, after all

Theseus is king
women weep; and they do

Antigone cannot bear her loss
and wishes to die also

Ismene thinks about the next meal

Theseus will return the daughters
to Thebes

Theseus is king

Antigone 3

Antigone, twice bereft

Polynices dead, decreed
naked, decreed undignified,
decreed open to the sky

first, some dust
on his corpse, naked, pink
and purple; remembered the sweetness
that came forth from
the lion
somewhere else
and wept for Polynices' smile
and lack of fur
he, the lion in steel and iron
nearly no threat in life, not really,
not to one who knew him,
still a threat in death

her hand fears rotting and the vultures
take their time

Creon punishes the living
by not allowing
the dead to hide
their shame

never a moment of doubt, Antigone
always a woman
who put her family
first

here, again, she has something to do

a second time she digs deeper
her hands furrow a bed
the crumbling earth like loose linen
the stones for a blanket
careless in their pillowing fall

I offered three times to the dead
I screamed
there must be time to mourn
you do not understand
I do it for myself, not
for him and honour, that
I may cover my sorrow

On visiting Sylvia Plath's grave

a spike of trees
handling
breath

perhaps she
ran into a
woolgatherer
who fleeced her
coatless

her mind picked
out in the coarse fluff
caught on twigs

the wind hollowing at
her back
urging her on

the poet's wife
(I mean, of course, the poet)

who committed suicide
and whose words
found comfort
where she
could

choking a rose
leaves red lines
on your palm

a moment of roulette
no excitement
just a dull, aching pull
downward

Mapping gender, by the river

I tried a compass
          got vertigo

I follow the signs
          the crow flies above me

no one looks at me along the rocks

I stripe and square the hill
          I think of putting my hand

along the valley
          sideways
          the outside edge of my hand

I can't ignore the mill chimney
          no longer used

I think of taking my other hand
          and running it cupped
down the bricks
          I would prefer lying in the grass, myself

to being so alone and exposed

if I occupy both hands thus

I will be stuck in this valley for ever

so I wipe my hands
          against my legs

and I walk free
          into the town

Myth

one hand holds open
the door
      another
his eyes
      the third
beckons beams

the ghosts of suffocation
march, ladies to the nipple,
biting their nails into blunt-edged instrument
      as all else fails to scratch
his surface.

      hiding behind shades is ok
as long as
Orpheus doesn't
turn his back.

Who was that other Greek
whose spurned lady
gave him a poisoned shirt
and left him to writhe
by the sea, as the cloth
burned into him.

It doesn't matter; the name;
his bones have already
      been used
for an anatomy lesson.

sacrificial — fire
keep away — no scorch

ashes on the sand blow
quenched into the water
he can weave a new cloth
out of bleached grains

Some male poets

they write poems about
the softness of our skin
the curve and softness
in our eye
the declivity of our waist
as we recline

we are their peace, their consolation

they do not write of the rage
quivering

we snuggle perfection in
the ball of our foot

our hair weaves
glowing by lamplight
as we wait for the step
on the step

they have not written of
the power in

we approach divinity in
our life-source
we are earth-mother
yearned for
absent muse
shed a silent tear for
missed and loved

we are their comfort, their inspiration

sometimes we are regretted
when we behave
like a jealous woman
and loved for
our jealousy which
shows our devotion

they have not written of

and when we have begun to
speak of it, limping
coarsely, our eyes
red with sleepless pyramids

they have written of us as
whores, devouring Liliths

and never as

On whether men can be feminists

if it is true
that women
have no sense of humour
(we can't tell a joke,
can't remember funny stories,
not like a witty bloke)

and if it is true
that feminists
of all women
especially
and particularly
have no sense of humour

then it must follow
from that —
assuming that God
gave all the wit to men —
it must follow
irrevocably
and incontrovertibly
that men
cannot
be feminists

QED

Love and the labour movement

the interim agreement allowed for
an impulse to touch;
feelings on the agenda,
intellectual stimulus
freedom to talk

it did not allow for
desire
obsession
passion
ecstasy

it was therefore
rational
in the long run

in the short run
they minuted
the moments

imagined
under
Any Other Business

and their eyes smoked
across a crowded
committee room:
we have not been ratified
and will not take
the risk
of a wildcat affair;
we are, after all
good
trade unionists

Reflection

the guiding thread; no
generalisations about man or woman
any distinctions are irrelevant,
the choice merely between images

at least, that's what it thought
until a beastie glared back from
the mirror; suddenly
back from the cradle jumped

the giant and Baba Yaga
in her three-legged chicken hut

and the pike who always got the perch

it all shudders so furiously
that no hand can steady it
for fear momentum
will disrupt the fingers

tiny tiny
pieces of glass
jagging in different parts
of the planet; jeering, but there's
no blood

she did suffer, the witch;
trying to peer round the looking
glass she forgot
someone was in the way

Maltese ferry

Mothers: women bypassed
by their men, their
children hang Tantalus over
the ferry rail

the boat slithers, its
belly clanging cars
(The Nuncio's shadow melts
somewhere)

in the bar the men clatter
their beer, on the
deck the children bear
with handsome indifference
their mothers' automaton
jackpots of good manners

the children
mimic the carelessness
of their fathers
boys and girls
no sturdy difference
in those kicking, swinging legs

while set back
from the sea
the women swim
in their draped black limbo
neither child
nor adult male

Gozo lacemakers

lace belies stone,
faces to the wall, no dust
on the dun-coloured linen

old ladies still weave
filigree dreams off
Fungus Rock; the inland sea
tickles the arid heights

a family squints into the shallow
salt pools, brushes white
crystals into heaps resting
against molten rock

sweet bitter tastes
prismatic in the sun

lava is a memory,
stone roots burned into the ground
snow flakes would not be
as kind

the mainland has been
adopted by machines: here
are still traces of
lace on stone

Geography

for some reason
sometimes
you remind me
of a seascape
(even as noisy)
your sentences
washed smooth
by a sea that
has visited
your shores
since eleven forty-two
a fleet second
compared to the history of the world
and light years
to a backwash
like myself

I hear you loudest
when you smile
and when you carry
someone else's baby
out of the hall
your third eye
noting your own nobility

on the striped carpet
your hair slaps
blonde waves
you push the sea back
your hands
blonde waves
heavy

your cheeks packed
with words
cross-legged
Olaf's daughters caressing
your calves
I lie, you warn us
and then you lie

and we believe you

Untitled 1

pieces
               fall   ing
  round   exhausting
  mine and his before time
  around us
  round us rounds
  us close

          hold

  look light,

          shield

  quiet glass apologies
  for breaking light
  scorching tomb pages backwards,
  calling dead words for dead
  against

          that touch? that breath?
balancing

Untitled 2

Our bodies held back
our minds held our bodies
back
held

          us

101

into suspension hovering
neatlessly between
grasping people-vices,
tell me the difference
between blood and madness;

cathedrals are built
around space
and what floating seems
is held,
and what may air be
is object-loved,
touched with tense time
knowing the invisible fruit
has seen roots,
will drink the earth.

Untitled 3

Tears haze tears, warm, filling
swelling a covenant of
We both do till all these things
us do.

follows

betrayal in the dark,
the lie, the half-light,
or murder at high noon, no
blood no bruise.

Water torture leaving no scars
save a gentle blush
telling where love has been.

The mad girls

the mad girls sit; reading
alone, their
mouths bared, their teeth
ache
the mad girl cannot get out of her
room; no one is in the street
                    and she is
afraid they will
hurt her

the mad girls have screamed
rhythmically —
you can see it
in their eyes
the mad girl no longer trusts her
love, never having called it that

the mad girls are pretty, the
mad girl evokes pity

the mad girl has hurt her hand on
lips
many times, not wanting any name or
condition to be put to it
the mad girls still laugh at the old jokes, the
mad girl consoles death in his quarantine

the mad girl rocks alone, the
mad girl
smiles, the
mad girl has learned her
own joke and is being
tickled to death by it

Willow pattern

tinkle over the edge   a porcelain dish
fell   damn it late

blue and white lovers
chasing across the bridge
what's he saying?
           'hurry up, silly girl, they'll
           catch us'

and she standing   look beyond
what she can see
           dropped him
           and no chivalry to pick up

tablecloth: best Irish linen, orange-dyed
a dead bluebottle (English)

imagine being the only people
on a plate

she cannot cross the bridge
and he waits

America

Calling the siren a liar didn't help the dead man
but neither did the siren
or the dead man the siren help.

She swam light-clear, high-peer in a car
boned with Republican health,
gleaned many beatings away
from red rebellion shades
turning to black water scrutiny's mourning.

Any black widow might martyr
her scrubbed steps, paying dust tribute
to collateral must. Where he ought
he never would, focusing on lines
was always always too much. And yet
stretching this routine across streets
increased fairness into torment, never
once doubting the flood or vicing
the versa beyond its ought.

The related uncles do not feel intimidated
by family threats;
their position agonises tenuousness,
love, a blind bone, it cannot break
for want of focus or frame.

Screaming quite accompanies steel-less
its switchback move, quits
bristling, bursts out-shaping that
distance, that far, that all everyone
that felt
that lingered piercing on level
cymbals, even stealing quite friends
into dead enemies.

Untitled 4

From now on we shall muffle
the sound of tears evaporating;
replace rather with a
crisp simplicity: mark me
my face a creased gargoyle
thirsting beyond rain. Gutter
snipe missed, army boots have weighed
themselves muddy
                    now   about
      turned
hunching khaki back to barracks

                    the colonel smells muffins burning

small in perspective's distance,
bunched, without the sound turned up,
granite pours into his hot glass
feet dissolving. Under the pavements
hornets buzz, waiting to sting
that delicate part of his instep
kept pure since birth

taken   trumpets fire, all   left
of the gas fields
                erupt into a blue horizon
and butter oozing through
these sad days

too fast to lick fingers
or use to grease the bolts into
aim

    where the sky
was weighing too hard
on a head studded
with steam

           engraving its
cheek
      on the pavement

Marriage end

slow   *divide*   now
       into future

                            edges age, fade
blurt

        falling
            feathers
dandelion fluff
        a dead cat
sleeping by the side
        of the road

        being alone
anyway, in the middle

        a   lone
all-one
     eyes are closed

this is the moment when
a fountain
        suddenly stopped
and silence floundered

in sunlight water dries
          and
I begin to hate definite articles

        they are always lying
        by roadsides
        eyes open under *the* lids

fur...   grey...
                  slowly
                        someone will come
                                  soon
and take us away

Untitled 5

I know three things in the world

two of them are you

third is your face
in the ivy outside my
window and the black
matt sequins on the sky

and the plainest of plain
things you said
reaching away to where the edges
were lit by night

I'm crowded
and they are all you

Untitled 6

my apologies
rasp fingernails on
your window

my blood in
your invisible
furrows

Untitled 7

in the middle of the night
people tell their dreams

and it is important, even
though there is never much
of an audience

Heaven

the swallow with a chunk
of chalk in his beak
is going to scrawl across the sky:

'I am an aeroplane.
And if you don't believe me,
come up here and check.'

Hopeful harbour

down at the quay
they're waiting
anchors high as hopes

waiting to push
the battleship potential
out to see

Twice sprung

crabapple
fingers;
      this year
      harvesting
      is difficult

            the crowded hydrangea
            has each its hand
            in its neighbour's
                        skull

Untitled 8

chickens keep crossing
the road, while I shout loudly
the bus leaves from here

Psychosoma speaks out

if you don't love me
when I'm ill
then you don't love me
then I'm ill

Untitled 9

catpad along;
                you're
another
        saw the colour of your
        fur last year

        still want to
        stroke you

Lullaby

She sang me to sleep
made sure I had her dreams
and then protested
when I awoke
from her nightmare

Old man

grabbing   in crisis

all your life you have lived
with rage

now a tear topples hatred, you become
a Samson fighting against
the scissors

somewhere an error of communication, wires
which never crossed, someone
forgot to touch wire ends

now you must mourn alone
black earth soiled your heart
sticky with bully's blood
steel sliced your semi-detached castle
away from the love of vellum
my illuminated letters just so much
compost, shivering brown in your stare

your misery
like a scorched ditch
after harvest

Argument

warm the bricks
peep hard through
the hard glass
oblong gaze through
the Venetian blinds
slat yourself
against the warm brick
rub your back, arch
your fair mind

I am still looking for you
looking out through
my hard black window
my share of the language
piling up around me

Untitled 10

thick ice   you
rib me
tickle the water drip along
my spine
mercury loves you
slipping silver   never was
so intangible a lover
never lost so intractable a joker
what you do not like
is that I like
my dreams much more than you

Hell

never seen such a slow day
never been
inside minutes
with such slothful ways
never crawled to heed
a leaden moment second by
crawling degree segmenting
slow motion's morale
cried screaming inside
one head or other
unheard, unread, unheeded
a red halo shadowing
her head, and blue
glows haunting his shoulder
I, circling silent and invisible
hear the crack of my arm
whipping, exaggerated,
low-timbre sounding
hounded away

Untitled 11

ripping the skin off a dead rabbit
but the image may disgust you;
it is an attempt, in the light of —
what I cannot send, and what
is mislaid — to fathom whether it
is a question of dredging the guts
in the knowledge of a new
generation; a new, re-generation;
whether it is even worth
speculation on the theory of the
image.
      Perhaps even this is too much,
too soon, too mislaid. Timing being a
fine thing
          when the image enters a
dream, at second remove, mirroring
faces behind glass
               wryness at the paper
flung aside to conceal itself or wrap
the mess
             so language is a matter of choice,
then, and time is as much language as cloak

the last access; many lists
a bare carcase
a pile of crumbs in the
corner of the bakery

and the hard irony
that having written this
I cannot send it
for the answer is not to be translated

Untitled 12

at various points wolves in
the snow make more sense.
Sleeping, they curl now, a warm
core between belly and tail, round
furs with clean banks between them

bound, we are bound together
by an accident of together
that a moment was real

after, the soft cocoons inside-out
blending red with the snow

and sometimes when the night
guts extra dark
one will stagger off and back
lips licked for dead fur
further
the fire of palm leaves
hands gloved, held out.
Only a beginning.

Untitled 13

I grope against

Infinity on a shoestring
Eternity testing time by pushing
me towards some other oblivion.

Meanwhile I must teach my son
to tie his laces

Homework

closed, face to the window

hands are thinking warm

       I can't see exactly where
the boy is reading,
dirty nails

       words are so important that
they count through the spelling

I am supposed to read each page
as it is finished and held out
to me   he knows why

       he sings tiredness   the
speckled leaves close for
the night.

       brushes fade the lavender
and in dark places

we are breathing together
in different rhythms

Birth

I have a child
I have another child
I had the first one first
and the second one second

But perhaps I over-simplify

I want some crisps

I can throw anything I like at you

I hate you

I'll move out and never come back
if I don't get my crisps NOW

WHEN I WANT
                    WAAAH
            AAGHAAA
                        kick crash hurt your heel, silly
heel
    aiming eyes just wide e —
                WAAAH   nough
to avoid the really sharp bits, like table corners

you can't come to my party
you're not my best friend any more
I won't let you be my MUMMY

and I still want my crisps
or a chocolate

I want a chocolate
                    go and get me one
I'll eat all my breakfast and I'll
never shout

and if you don't GIVE ME A CHOCOLATE
I'll never speak to you again

I WANT

do you know my friend Neil kicked me
and pushed me over but I punched him and
he
    CRIED . . .

I'm very big and strong

and I'm going out to play now

can I have an apple, Mummy?

Episode of an angry mother

I have shouted at them five times today

and each time felt worse afterwards

because I am a mother
why should I be my own warder?

because I am responsible
why must I be rewarded
with a nightly curfew?

I do not enjoy myself much

when I go out I
think of the clock, the baby-sitter
the cost
the breakfast
the knowledge that I will be shouted
awake by fights of happy noises
of loud playing

they are beautiful and I love them

my day has iron brackets round four
o'clock, my evenings barely exist
I need my tele, my knitting, my books,
my work

but I need people too, I need the
freedom not to be responsible for a
short time

I am not very nice

I have little patience with other people
they are all children
who demand or contradict
and I am tired of being a mother

your eyes are
puzzled, you think, what a difficult
person, so tense, so over-intense about
her reactions, what a *difficult* person

and you draw back because I am slightly
too shrill, too breathless, as though I
have no time or calm

I have no time or calm; I have to get back
my baby-sitter is taking O-levels, I
have not the time to sit over a drink or have the
luxury of missing the last tube home

No

I don't want it *instead*

but under my breath I swear at you,
you who proclaim in actions your irresponsibility

for other people
while campaigning for the ultimate
responsibility of all of us for each other

(we were all babies
we all get ill and need
cups of tea
and comfort still)

I make you feel guilty?
you make me feel inadequate,
'just' a housewife

hug your freedom tighter, girlie,
because when you have your babies
I won't be there

I might be so bitter
so twisted, so nasty
that I may even rub
my bitten claws together
at your moments of protesting imprisonment

and if you have no kids? well, as
you grow older, in whatever freedom,
I will gloat to myself
that I have learned
even as I fight against it
the meaning of continuing responsibility

so if we're still playing the old game
I'm okay, Jill, I pull rank —
to myself as well as to you
and watch you pull rank with
your independence, your right
to choose

I am still a mother and you are not and
neither I nor you will let you forget it

bitter?

well, *you* stick your tongue out at the
wind of history
and see what tastes get
deposited there

London airport

gone in the air, the bird

on the plane, departure point
always a fine line between
too early and too late, waved goodbye before they
left, never got the moment quite right,
such a fine line between presence
and past, such a quick
move between now you see it, now
you don't, times and spaces back
where you come from the same (give or take
a change in air current or two)

the parts flow into reason's
corners and you can lay it all
out in order and still it
doesn't make a sense that
corresponds the mind's working
to the feeling

        so they have (poets)
tried for centuries to find greater meaning
in the event than
momentary sadness; what are we to project?
'that all must go' (in death or international
travel; define the difference)
'that nothing stays in one place'
'that change is life's rich source of
tragedy and happiness for God's sake'

such mechanisms are rusty; rasp as you listen
are no longer in accord with the event and its
history
        still holding onto the rift between what has
actually happened and the emptiness, let us reject
some of the old means and grope towards a
new accuracy:
        a domestic division means two children

move between two homes. The symmetry is fitful,
the feeling a protest at unnecessary pain.
The answer?

Make sure no more unions of this kind
(you know its name)
take place; build houses of many people
so no child need leave one home for another
and cross deserts on the way.
Make all houses big and make them homes.
Make all people lovers and parents, make one
word mean that. Make
unions of rivers so that no one can tell
where one ends and another begins and
then stand at airports and wave goodbye and
smile into the tea; time and space are to
be welcomed and crossed, not feared

'how' is another poem

Christmas, 1978

2 pm: two degrees
6 pm: six floury flakes fly
              across my windscreen
10 pm: clouds of snowdust
across the roads
flying headlights
outside my window
a spider's web
half whitened in
the wind's path

spider tried hard
said ay ay snow's up
weave away, lad,
not much time

11 pm: snow clinging to
the road
car slithers
back and forth
leaves curvy zigzag

spider pokes
his head
through the middle
sniffs around
with three legs

fuck this
for a lark
I'm off under
the oil tank
out of the wind

adam snowed under
with excitement
the wind blowing
his mind
would run outside
fling his clothes off
let the snow coat him
his legs filigree white

his head through
the top
scooping snowballs
with his eyes
his fingers splayed
feather white
white,
like sugar
wet
like melted sugar

12 pm: adam snores the sleep
of the teenage just
from beneath
the oil tank
the spider sees
his web blown

fuck that one
for a lark
set to weaving a
safer home
less available
to skies' caprices

so what if it's five minutes
past midnight
since when
did spiders
get double time
for sunday?

Chocolate egg

my chocolate egg
of a boy
silver and blue laughing
wrapping you
nestling over your shell
dark and bitter
with sharp sugar suchard
eyelashes
a mouth
that any orange
lush segment would juice
to be chewed by

no more baby
no more lying there
soft, for me to unpeel
no more milky curl
of your mouth in sleep

now a firebrand
melting your own anger
lifting heavy weights
a real bicep
lurking there
all these years

no more easy kisses
no more easy
scoop you up
under your soft middle
in one hand

instead
'hullo, shortie'
as you whirl your new height
in from school
my footprints
disappear in yours

leaving us
our pet names
hunger and thirst
and a tall
lanky you
pouncing, worrying,
questing, desperate
for the unpacked shopping bag
the final secret
the love of your life
your favourite of all time
your own coated darling
your chocolate egg

Crafty

my son is becoming a spider
let me explain

he has legs everywhere, especially in
his mind's eye
he has spun a web around childhood
held it fast
and then decamped
to a safe distance

he has climbed
the Matterhorn from bed
curled up
and slept in its shadow

he has crawled across my carpet
running too fast
for my arms to reach him
he has hidden
himself in his own recesses
and as I look up
all I can see
are legs, legs, legs
running away from me
so fast
they leave no prints

I am having to revise
my opinion of
the arachnids I meet
around the house

My mother's funeral in Waltham Abbey

the gold band
plays its roll
across Europe
for the last time

trundles on the metal
wheels, wooden planks
slat the black metal
the black cloth covers
the wood, cheap wood
it will crumble gracefully
in time

dank greenness
more polluted than
Poland's fields in 1919
one pogrom or another
no nice distinction
but you left then,
you trundled on
any wheels
you let the wheels carry you
away, across, perhaps
to safety
certainly to the mud
to hack roads out of
the sand
to cook beans in
old petrol cans
round, you rose with
pride from sepia
(we can still make copies
of you)

you can't stand in the middle
of Europe any more
you can't stand
on the dunes
between Tel Aviv and Ramat Gan
any more
this time we all
followed you
across your Europe
for the last time

I slept in my clothes
last night
just so you'll know
I think of you
sleeping in yours

After the Renaissance

it has rained all winter
unending
I have given up trying to wash the stone free of mud
the clogged earth outside
is a curtain of sound
no-one remembers silence
it is a past age

the rain swirls
gusts with wind
soaks the backs of your legs
clings stickily through the wool
until your skin is permanently damp
and you begin to melt
into the air, your body's water
straining to return to heaven
the heaven's water flowing
in through your pores
until you are nothing but
traces of silt on the floor

the devil's trill is the only thing
that can keep the rain at bay
the insistent, repeated note, vying with
the insistent beat of the rain

the devil cannot hear my voice
the devil drowns me with his trill
the devil knows the secret of the tides
the devil knows how to switch the clouds off
the devil knows how to draw aside the curtain of water
and let the sun through

the devil has cheated me
the devil trills the rain outside
and inside
the devil uses me
drawing his repeated presence across me
forcing me to give him voice
in the note after the note after the note

my fingers are in someone else's hand
my arm moves to someone else's command
the rest of me waits
for a resolution
that never comes

Where does class go in the winter time?

we scions of the wooden spoon
found we had to
took years to
spit the sawdust out of our mouths
and curl our tongues
into the bowl of sound
round and stretching vowels kneaded
into completed consonants
which took us to
those we wanted to hear us —
or so we thought
for thought comes easy
and in any accent you fancy

we scions of the wooden spoon
must spit the coal dust
and the tailor's chalk
and wipe
the black and the white
from the corners
of our mouths

Music will out

why he played
was because the band
was locked in his room

the music dripped from his fingers
and clogged the draughts
round the window
and under the door

he liked the look of
black vinyl
because it was safe

until one day
faces smiled from between
the grooves
and forced him out through the keyhole
backwards through the frets
and onto the stage
where the band played on
and he was finally on
rain chords and all

you cannot string me
tighter than I sharpen myself
he sang

In the sixties

in the sixties, I
left home
got a degree
got married
had two children
separated
started writing
became a feminist
became a socialist

in the sixties, I
wore very, very short mini-skirts
tried to sit carefully, so as not to show my knickers
wore lots of mascara
worried that my nose would shine red through my make-up
(which it did) when I had a cold (which was often)
was told I 'had the best legs in London'
learned to jive
was very snooty about the early Beatles
got hooked on Buddy Holly and the Everly Brothers
wore contact lenses

in the sixties, I
was terrified of the world outside my home
couldn't wait to leave home
was terrified of the world outside University
fell in love

in the sixties, I
was the first girl from my (mixed) grammar school to be
at (go up to) Cambridge University
in the sixties I first felt the shock of not having the right
accent or enough money
in the sixties I was going to be Sarah Bernhardt (with
two legs)
in the sixties I found it very hard to sit still in libraries
in the sixties I packed plastic potties in my summer holi-
days (sorry, vacations)
in the sixties I delivered the post at Christmas
in the sixties I fell in love with oh so many desirable people
of all possible sexes and did nothing (conscious) about it

in sixties' Cambridge
I acted in dozens of plays
directed one
loved the buildings
was upset by the snobbery
met people who are still friends
met people who are now famous
for the first time ever met people whose parents were
divorced and was amazed to find they were still whole
people
played the recorder secretly and very fast in my college
room
played the clarinet publicly and was never happy with my
embouchure

in sixties' Cambridge
I fell in love for absolutely real
and lots of things were done about it
most of them wonderful
and some of them appalling

in the sixties, I
tried hard to be a good wife and mother (honest)
cooked from Carrier, Deighton and David (still got the
books to prove it)
had a Mary Quant haircut
wore hand-me-down Biba dresses swapped for books with
one of the girls who worked there
entertained George Steiner and Anthony Burgess to dinner, followed by Jean Shrimpton and Heathcote Williams
(to name but a few)

in the sixties, you see, I
was the wife of an up-and-coming young publishing
executive
we went to parties; despite having top-notch educational
credentials, I still had the wrong accent and was 'just' a
housewife
in the sixties I was, as I was in the forties, fifties, seven-
ties and eighties, the daughter of Jewish Polish-Russian
immigrants

so

in the sixties, I
fell in love seriously twice more, with my sons Adam and
Ivan
in the sixties, I
began to discover that the love affair you have with your
children lasts forever

in the sixties, I
went to see the Living Theatre at the Round House and
La Mama in Notting Hill

in the sixties, I
met Richard and Louise and Marsha and the *Oz* lot and
thought they were something else, and went to UFO and
dazzled mine eyes on graphic magazines and saw my first
pornographic film, and envied people who slept around a
lot and wondered how they did it and never found out,
but then I was still 'just' a housewife, albeit with the
'best legs in London', though Louise's were pretty hot
competition, I must say

in the sixties, I
lusted over more legs than you've had hot dinners

in the sixties, I
tried to smoke pot (man) but couldn't because I have
asthma and couldn't inhale the smoke

in the sixties, I
had a hot line in hash fudge, courtesy of the corruption
of a recipe from Florence Greenberg's *Jewish Cookery
Book* (I bet she'd never heard of Alice B. Toklas)
in the sixties, I
finally learned to love the psychedelic Beatles
finally learned to use Tampax
tried the pill, the coil and the cap (God, what a drag)
visited my parents regularly every week and shouted at
my father (he shouted first, honest)

in the sixties, I
was ill a lot
stopped playing the recorder
had never heard of the viol

the sixties
were full of people I didn't sleep with
joints I didn't smoke
plays I wasn't in

the sixties were
when everything
and everyone
got stirred up

the sixties
were full
of unrequited lusts

the sixties was a time when many people went to pot
except for me
I did not

during the sixties
I yearned
a lot

Haiku 1

my son lying ill
hurt through no fault of his own
loving the hot sun

Haiku 2

do not talk to your-
self, because if you do, then
people will listen

Haiku 3

remember that to
be at home is to revere
being there, at home

Hard work 1

wherever a card fails
another harps a string
of coincidences
how you avoid
a carping hand
involves muscle
and endeavour
like a sandwich
floating on air

Hard work 2

lightly iced
and spiced
I sit and
flex my syllables
into raspberry glasses
and leafy mint fronds

look
I've done the crossword

The lady and the unicorn

I am the beast
who sees you
stroke my fine white fur

                once I ran as swift as the deer

who am I

                once I rode the four winds

my body is white
my head is red
my eyes are blue

                their strong backs between my
                thighs

who am I   who am I

I run faster than the moon
dapple my shadow as I run

                now I sit
                my skirt in my lap

who am I

                my head to one side

I love the lion as he roars

                I love the lion as he roars

catch me as I chew his flesh

                        I love my hair in the breeze
                        who am I

who am I

I am the beast
who lies down in your lap

                        once a beast lay in my lap

who am I

                        and then I could no longer run
                        swift as the deer
                        who am I

let me lay my head in your lap

                        now I speak the truth
                        soft as the wind

lady

                        now I hear the whispers
                        on the wind
                        as I speak the truth

my horn in your lap

                        who am I to speak the truth

who am I

                        who can no longer hear
                        the wind

to love you
lady

who lies with the truth

whom no-one has loved   whom no-one has loved

Fire and Ice: the world turned upside down

One

Today the world is turned upside down
today autumn creeps between stone and leaf
today I am haunted by a memory
a memory of carnival
a memory of May creeping between leaf and stone
into October

I remember Bacchus, the God of wine, riding through the
city
on a cart drawn by white panthers
I remember a wedding with a bear as the groom
a fish buried with full military honours
a horse galloping backwards

I remember cities in the sky
the sun and moon turning cartwheels in the piazza
I remember the world turned upside down

I remember carnival

in the cold sun of a winter morning
you somersaulted across the piazza
a rose between your teeth

you bowed
you handed me the flower
you danced away

a white suit
red ribbons on your shoes
a ruff around your neck

you wanted to play Piero to my Colombina

where did you go
where can I find you

today I rise and dress in a white Piero suit
and go to the city in search of you

today cheats are honest and liars tell the truth
today high voices sing low and low voices high
today the minutes move slowly
and the hours flash by
today ice burns and fire chills
today the world is turned upside down

Two

today play begins in earnest
vagabonds and beggars are feasted by nobles
men of the church swear
women from the palaces roam the streets

carnival, fat and festive,
joins with austerity, thin and grim
they wear saucepans for helmets
and fight with spoons and forks

the city is a theatre
and every street a stage

today oranges fly through the streets
today the air is thick with the scent of rose water

and we, the strolling players
prance and dance
in our white and black caps
our coloured clothes
tied with ribbons
hung with bells
lace ruffs
floppy sleeves
buttons shaped like bears

the streets are full of Pieros and Colombinas

today I am dressed as Piero
today I search for my double
my other self
for the Piero who gave me a rose at carnival

Three

you run before me
turning and twisting
through piazzas
between towers
along narrow, twisting streets
you slip between carts
piled high with melons and golden peppers

you dart in and out of the sun
you catch the dappled, flecked shadows
of green and pink churches
you leap over the sewers
you run on light feet
you catch at bales of bright silk on the market stalls
you tease past barrels of corn and
children playing dice on the cobbles

I chase you
I catch the edge of your white, flowing shirt
it tears
I hold a piece of you in my hand

Four

the Duchess of Ferrara has a company of strolling players
the Duke of Mantua has a company of strolling players
the Duke and the Duchess have made a pact
the companies are to be united

a marriage has been arranged
between the Piero of one company
and the Colombina
of the other company

the goddess Minerva descends from the highest star
to offer her beauty and intelligence
for the glory of the city

for two cities are to be united
through the marriage of
Colombina and
Piero

Five

how will I know you?

Six

at carnival
I remember
the army
marching into the vanquished city
two hundred knights on foot
Swiss guards
men armed with steel halberds
pikes and lances
officers in helmets
with thick, waving plumes

five thousand Swiss guards playing the rebec
five thousand Swiss infantry
three thousand cavalry
in engraved armour
with brocade cloaks
and velvet banners embroidered with gold

I remember
the dance of the fighting men
the Gascon infantry
the Breton archers
the crossbowmen

a long way from you, Piero
in your white suit
the ruff around your neck
red ribbons on your shoes

Seven

during carnival you find what you have lost
and lose what you have found

in the back streets
children play hide and seek
in and out of the deep, dark doorways

I see a child folded in a doorway
the child wears a white suit
a ruff around a fat pink neck
red ribbons round the ankles

the child peels an orange
the zest paints the child's hands orange
the child sucks the fruit and
the juice rolls down the suit
a runnel of orange blood
the peel is sucked dry
the child flings the peel into the street
and runs before me

during carnival boys become girls and girls become boys

we salute one another as we pass

two Pieros
not man
not woman
not child

Eight

an open window
a canopied bed stands on a raised platform
ready for lovers to sleep naked
beneath the linen sheets
breathing in air made sweet by the scent of herbs
burning slowly in pierced globes
hanging from the ceiling
whitewashed walls
plain wooden table
tapestries unpacked from dusty wooden chests
silver taken from a locked cupboard
glass and majolica

not for us the Lenten spinach
cooked in salt water
not for us the herrings pickled in salt and vinegar
for us a meal that breaks all the rules
boiled capon
roast chicken
guinea fowl
turtle dove and peacock

rice cooked in milk, with almonds
sugar and honey
pine kernels
jellies of almond milk
coloured with saffron
made in the shapes of animals
made in the shapes of
Piero and Colombina

Nine

the bow strokes the strings of the viol
and reason is killed gently
gently your eyes spell the death of reason

I shiver with fever
I burn with the chill
of your gaze
I fly with the courage of ice
I cover every inch of the streets and the squares
without moving my feet

my hands are bound
my feet are rooted to the ground
my tongue is silent
and I am free

will I find you among the spiced ginger
will I find you among the oranges
the cinnamon and cloves
the dates and the olives
will I find you between the frets of the viol?

Ten

devils throw fireworks at the crowd
shadows lengthen and quicken
lanterns and candles
flickering shadows run along the walls
desire runs through the streets

fountains flow with wine

the Palazzo blazes with light
at the ball
everything is allowed
everyone can seem to be what they most desire

Eleven

the musicians are ready
the world processes
the simplest gesture is a ceremony

with whom shall I dance?

the courtier in his red breeches
high boots of Spanish leather
doeskin jersey
black velvet jewelled cap

with the God Bacchus
with the goddess Minerva

Piero, where are you?

Twelve

a child in a corner
a child in a white suit
a twirl of orange peel
hanging from one tired hand

out
from between the strings
out
to meet the music

your hand burns in mine
like ice
our eyes scorch
the painted room

candles flicker on the walls
the wind is strong and silent

a single leaf blows in through the window
it falls on the child's white suit
the child's hand closes on the leaf

silk and brocade
cloth of gold
silver thread
weaves the music round
and round us

the orange peel
twirls crimson
on a dead leaf
on a child's white suit

the candles bloom
and silk tumbles down before the windows
brocade warms the walls
fur steals over the stone

now I dance
now I dance
with a white suit
that eats orange peel
the wine is sweet and strong
and red in the candle light
flames with cloves and cinnamon
sharp with orange peel

Thirteen

once upon a time
the Duchess of Ferrara
had a band of strolling players

no-one was what they seemed
no-one seemed to be what they were
a marriage was arranged
between
Piero
and Colombina

they did not meet
until the music played

Fourteen

I lost you once
in and out of the sun
between green and pink churches
wrapped in bales of silk
tripping over children playing dice
and eating oranges

today as the leaves of autumn
swirl and tease
with the red ribbons
of memory
I remember
carnival
and spring

a white suit
a torn white suit
red ribbons on your shoes
light in the sky
dawn

fire and ice

in a corner sleeps
a child in a white suit

York: a cantata for two voices

Prologue

in the city of York

        in the city of York

there is more than one story

        do not

I tell of two cities

        tell

I tell two stories

        do not

two stories tell the city of York

        lament

where cold stone cries

        in the city of York

where fire bleeds

        do not

where paper smoulders

        lament

where the knife cuts

        tell

I tell the city of York

        the city of York

and its story

        its stories

The first story

In the one thousand one hundred
and eighty-ninth year from the
fulness of time
        did the sun shine

Richard, the son of Henry the Second,
that most illustrious king of England,
succeeded to the throne upon the death
of his father
        did it rain

consecrated king at London

> did the leaves fall

on the third day of September

> and did it rain

from some superstitious precaution,
the king forbids us to enter the church
while he is being crowned or to enter
the palace where the banquet is being
held

> or did the sun shine

and the people begin to crowd in

> and did the leaves fall

we mingle with the crowd and are
thus driven within

> in rain or sun

The second story

sticks and stones and fists

> wet leaves and sun

stone walls will not take fire but
wooden roofs will

> drying, dry

the sky lit up until sunset

> the dying year

The first story

the new king, of a lofty and fierce
disposition, was filled with
indignation and grief that such
events had occurred

> falls

the king, after the slaughter,
establishes peace by proclamation

> and dies

164

the king, after the slaughter,
gives provinces to his own relations

and falling

the king of England, after the slaughter,
makes ready to set out with the king of
France towards Jerusalem

dies

The second story

the king of the Scots pays Richard,
son of Henry, ten thousand marks
of silver

in the city of York

the bishop of Durham gives the king
whatever he has accumulated and
receives an earldom to add to his
bishopric

in this city of York

I would sell London also, if I could
find a suitable purchaser, says
the king

in the city of York

it is said that he will never return
to this country, for he is already
broken down and languid through
the premature and immoderate use
of arms in which he has indulged
more than is prudent from his youth

the city of York

The first story

some say his system is corrupted
by an ague which he has endured
for a long time

                     the people are divided into
                                   two cities

note the paleness of his face and
the swelling of his limbs

                               I tell of two cities

more than one hundred issues on
his body to carry off the corruption
of the humours

                            did it rain or did it shine

The second story

the king crossed over to Normandy
before the solemnities of Christmas

                           a city builds its own walls

The first story

there is, upon the public road to
London, a town called Dunstaple

                            a city makes itself
                               in its own image

there, certain persons happen to be
looking up at the sky

                            did the rain cease

and there they see

                            did the sun fall

the banner of the Lord and joined
to it the figure of a man crucified

                            did the city divide

and then the banner and the
figure part and there is a space
of air between them

              did the city divide to rule

The second story

Richard, the illustrious king of
England, and the king of France,
confirm their oaths of mutual
alliance and brotherly love

              who will rule the divide

The first story

in the city of Lynn
and at Stamford
and in the county of York

              make the city in its own image

many people take an oath
together against us

              stone

vision of fire in the dark

              upon stone

an armed band wielding iron

              stone

husbands, wives, children, swept away

              will not burn

entreat the governor of the royal
castle for mercy

              brittle beams burn

the governor leaves the castle and
is not permitted to enter again

              whom does the fire trust

167

the governor of the county gives
orders that the castle be attacked

                                    fire does not trust stone
bands of armed men from city
and country surround the castle

                                    walls crumble like paper
too late to regret the order

                                            we forget

The second story

several days pass

                                            the strong stand
                                            and hurl stones
                                            on those below
stones pulled out of the walls
of the interior

                                            we remember
a hermit urges on the fatal
work with loud shouts

                                    I may forget but
                                    I never forgive
it comes to pass that a large
stone falls from above and he
is crushed and expires

                                    I may forgive but
                                    I never forget

The first story

there is among us a certain elder,
a most famous doctor of the law
who comes from countries
beyond the sea

168

since we ought to prefer a
glorious death to an infamous life,
it is plain we ought to choose
the most honourable and easy
kind of death

                            the strong have
                               eyes of fire

many embrace this fatal advice

                               eyes of fire

others find this discourse hard

                               eyes of fire

and retreat

                             heart of stone

the roof is set on fire while the
knives are prepared

                     someone has bad dreams

the roof is set on fire while the
knives are prepared

                               my child

the roof is set on fire

                            look, we dance on
                            the warm stone

while

                         look how fast we turn

the knives

                          look how fast the
                    world turns and turns

are prepared

                     turn your face to mine

the roof is set

                         look, we can dance
                          on the future

the knives are set

                      the sun on the stone

                the stone beneath the sun

              our time has come, my child

a house filled with a cloud

                                    my child, oh, my child

The second story

next morning we stand on the
battlements

                                    eyes shell light

next morning we throw the dead
bodies over the battlements

                              dark husks darkness

next morning we pray for charity

                                    eyes wax still

next morning, when we come out,
we are received on the point of the sword

The first story

after the slaughter, they proceed
to the cathedral church

                                    did it rain

there they compel the wardens
to deliver the acknowledgements
of the debts deposited there

                                 was there sun

the papers are committed to the
flames in the midst of the church

                              did the leaves grow

The second story

the act committed at York is
reported to the king beyond the seas

                                    did the paper
                                    wrap the stone

he is indignant and enraged,
not only on account of the
treason against his royal
majesty, but because whatever
the Jews possessed appertains
to the treasury

did the stone
crush the knife

an army proceeds to York

did the fire
heat the stone

the principal ringleaders flee
to Scotland

paper

knife

stone

The first story

in the following year, in the one
thousand and one hundred and
ninetieth year from the fulness
of time, the illustrious kings of
France and England commenced
their journeys to Jerusalem

stone

paper

knife

The second story

a lullaby for a dead child

                               stone

a lullaby to wake the dead

                               paper

a lullaby for us

                               knife

does the lullaby ask why

               the paper wraps the stone
              the stone sharpens the knife
               the knife folds the paper

I might

                     my hand on my face

learn to

                     I might learn to

learn

                           learn

to grow

                         to grow

Acknowledgements

Gardens of Eden Revisited is an updated version of my Selected Poems. It includes most of the earlier volume, *Gardens of Eden* (Hutchinson), which was itself drawn from three earlier collections, *Gardens of Eden* (Journeyman), *Upbeat* (Journeyman) and *Touch Papers* (Allison and Busby). Individual poems have appeared in *Only Poetry, Writing Women, Gallery, Tribune, Spare Rib, The Little Magazine*, and many anthologies including *The New British Poetry,* ed. Gillian Allnutt, Fred D'Aguiar, Ken Edwards and Eric Mottram (Paladin); *A Picnic of Poetry*, ed. Anne Harvey (Blackie); *Ain't I a Woman*, ed. Ilona Linthwaite (Virago); *Life Doesn't Frighten Me At All*, ed. John Agard (Heinemann); *In the Sixties*, ed. Sara Maitland (Virago) and *The Dybbuk of Delight*, ed. Sylvia Paskin and Sonja Lyndon (Five Leaves). A play for two voices, based on the 'Gardens of Eden' sequence was broadcast on Radio 4, with music by Michael Nyman, and starring Miriam Margolyes and Maureen Lipman.

The new work included here includes two longer poems which are about, and are, music. *Fire and Ice* was first written under the title *Ben Venga Maggio*, as a script to dovetail with a sequence of Italian Renaissance carnival music, which was first broadcast on Radio 3, with music played by Musica Antiqua of London. The programme was runner-up at the Innsbruck Early Music Festival and was nominated for the Prix Italia and the Sony Radio awards. *York: a cantata for two voices* was commissioned by the Clifford's Tower Commemoration Committee, drawing on contemporary late-medieval sources. The music was by Malcolm Singer. The voices (one sung, one spoken) are contrapuntal.

MW
January 1999

Also available from Five Leaves

The Art of Blessing the Day: Poems on Jewish Themes
by Marge Piercy
0 907123 47 3,156pp, paperback, £7.99

Written in Bone: Early Poems
by Marge Piercy
0 907123 97 X, 156pp, paperback, £7.99

The Dybbuk of Delight: An Anthology of Jewish Women's Poetry
ed. by Sonja Lyndon and Sylvia Paskin
0 907123 57 0, 236pp, paperback, £9.99
Published in association with the European Jewish Publication Society

Laughing All the Way
by Liz Cashdan
0 907123 46 5, 72pp, paperback, £5.99

The Slow Mirror and Other Stories: New Fiction by Jewish Writers
ed. by Sonja Lyndon and Sylvia Paskin
0 907123 81 3, 230pp, paperback, £9.99
Published in association with the European Jewish Publication Society

The Vanished Shtetl: Paintings by Stanislaw Brunstein
ed. by Ross Bradshaw
0 907123 87 2, 52pp, paperback, £9.99
Published in association with the European Jewish Publication Society